SOUTH WALES RAILWAYS
AT THE GROUPING

(Overleaf) Cardiff Riverside Station

SOUTH WALES RAILWAYS
AT THE GROUPING

by

BRIAN J. MILLER

1986

D. BROWN AND SONS LIMITED

COWBRIDGE

© 1986 Brian J. Miller

ISBN 0 905928 55 5

DESIGNED AND PRINTED IN WALES BY
D. Brown & Sons Ltd., Bridgend, Mid Glamorgan.

CONTENTS

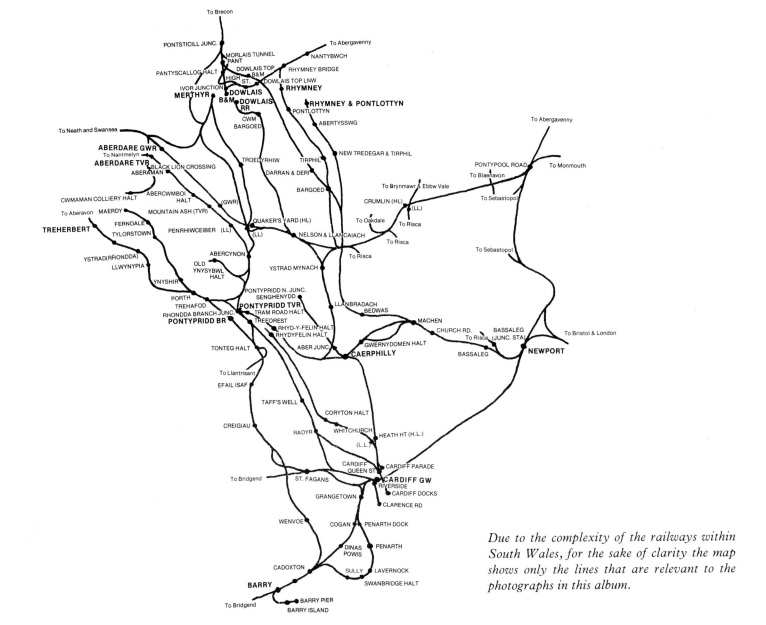

To Brecon

PONTSTICILL JUNC.

To Abergavenny

NANTYBWCH

MORLAIS TUNNEL
PANT
PANTYSCALLOG HALT
DOWLAIS TOP B&M
RHYMNEY BRIDGE
HIGH ST.
DOWLAIS TOP LNW
IVOR JUNCTION
MERTHYR
DOWLAIS B&M
DOWLAIS RR
RHYMNEY

RHYMNEY & PONTLOTTYN
PONTLOTTYN

CWM BARGOED
ABERTYSSWG

To Neath and Swansea

ABERDARE GWR
To Nantmelyn
ABERDARE TVR
BLACK LION CROSSING
ABERAMAN
TROEDYRHIW
TIRPHIL
NEW TREDEGAR & TIRPHIL

To Abergavenny

PONTYPOOL ROAD
To Monmouth

DARRAN & DERI
BARGOED
To Blaenavon

CWMAMAN COLLIERY HALT
ABERCWMBOI HALT
(GWR)
CRUMLIN (HL)
(LL)
To Sebastopol

To Aberavon
MAERDY
MOUNTAIN ASH (TVR)
To Brynmawr & Ebbw Vale
To Sebastopol
TREHERBERT
FERNDALE
PENRHIWCEIBER (LL)
QUAKER'S YARD (HL)
To Oakdale
To Risca
TYLORSTOWN
(LL)
NELSON & LLANCAIACH
YSTRAD(RHONDDA)
LLWYNYPIA
ABERCYNON
To Risca
To Risca
YNYSHIR
OLD YNYSYBWL HALT
YSTRAD MYNACH
To Sebastopol
PORTH
PONTYPRIDD N. JUNC.
TREHAFOD
SENGHENYDD
RHONDDA BRANCH JUNC.
PONTYPRIDD TVR
LLANBRADACH
PONTYPRIDD BR
TRAM ROAD HALT
BEDWAS
TREFOREST
MACHEN
RHYD-Y-FELIN HALT
CHURCH RD.
BASSALEG
RHYDYFELIN HALT
To Risca
(JUNC. STA)
To Bristol & London
TONTEG HALT
ABER JUNC
GWERNYDOMEN HALT
BASSALEG
NEWPORT
CAERPHILLY
To Llantrisant
EFAIL ISAF
TAFF'S WELL
CORYTON HALT
CREIGIAU
RADYR
WHITCHURCH
HEATH HT (H.L.)
(L.L.)
CARDIFF QUEEN ST
CARDIFF PARADE
To Bridgend
ST. FAGANS
CARDIFF GW
RIVERSIDE
GRANGETOWN
CARDIFF DOCKS
CLARENCE RD
WENVOE
COGAN
PENARTH DOCK
DINAS POWIS
PENARTH
CADOXTON
SULLY
LAVERNOCK
SWANBRIDGE HALT
BARRY
To Bridgend
BARRY PIER
BARRY ISLAND

Due to the complexity of the railways within South Wales, for the sake of clarity the map shows only the lines that are relevant to the photographs in this album.

INTRODUCTION

One of the most interesting periods in the history of the railways of South Wales was during the years 1921 to 1923 which encompassed the Grouping of the various Companies active in the region by the Great Western Railway, a Company that was despised by the majority of Companies it now took under its wing. The new owners tried enforcing their authority upon these railways that had been a thorn in the flesh of the GWR for many years, but met with little initial success and some old customs and traditions took many years to die.

About this time, a Mr. E. T. Miller (no relation to the author) who, it is believed, was the Secretary of the Railway Club at the time, appears to have visited South Wales on two occasions during the summers of 1921 and 1922, seemingly to view the Pre-Grouping Companies on the first visit and the GWR on the latter, taking a unique series of photographs of the stations, junctions and halts in the area.

It has been the author's good fortune to be able to purchase the original glass plate negatives of these two visits which are reproduced herein. There were at least three other photographs taken by Mr. E. T. Miller during these vacations, but the glass plate negatives have been severely damaged by a previous owner; luckily, 71 still survive to this day.

Many of the locations that are shown no longer exist, while those that are still used by British Rail bear little resemblance to when they were in private ownership; and it is the purpose of this album to try to illustrate what the railway scene was like in South Wales over sixty years ago. Comparisons can be made of the various styles of architecture, signalling and working that were adopted by the various companies to whom wealth meant the movement of coal.

Instead of putting the prints in alphabetical order, it was thought better to group them into Companies and complement them with maps appertaining to the area. This should enable the reader to imagine what it was like to travel by train in South Wales all those years ago, when the area was still alive with industry.

BRIAN J. MILLER
Barry 1986

DEDICATION

This book is dedicated to my wife Beti who somehow managed to keep our sons out of my hair, and my coffee cup full, during the compilation of this album.

ALEXANDRA (NEWPORT & SOUTH WALES) DOCKS & RAILWAY

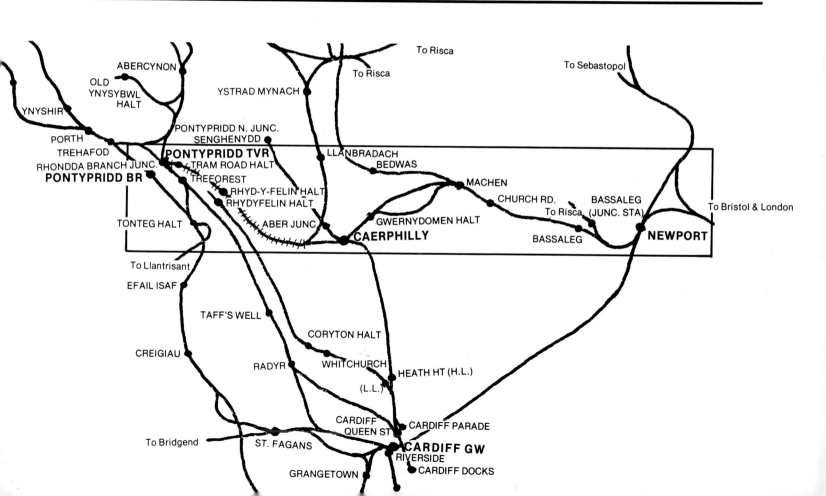

1 RHYD-Y-FELIN HALT

Viewed looking in a north-westerly direction towards Pontypridd with a Caerphilly bound train about to enter the small sleeper built halt. The engine is ADR No. 14, a former GWR '517' Class 0-4-2T, and is seen as rebuilt by Hawthorn, Leslie & Co. in 1919, with the cab backplate mounted on the top rear lip of the bunker. The train is made up of a converted railmotor and a former Barnum & Bailey coach, this was normal practice by ADR standards. Signalling on the ADR was by McKenzie & Holland. Rhyd-y-Felin Halt, to which the GWR added (High Level), was 1½ miles from Pontypridd, other halts between Caerphilly and Pontypridd were Nantgarw, Groeswen, Upper Boat, Dynea, Treforest, Glyntaff and Pontypridd Tram Road.

2 PONTYPRIDD TRAM ROAD HALT

Viewed looking in a westerly direction towards PC & N Junction, the Pontypridd Station of the Taff Vale Railway being to the right of this junction. The line from Pontypridd Tram Road to Caerphilly was double throughout but, for most of its route, the gradient was against loaded trains. Trains from Caerphilly originally ran into Pontypridd Station, but the ADR put a stop to this as they were not prepared to pay the TVR's junction and station charges, after which, the ADR services terminated at Tram Road Halt. Unusually, there was no cross-over at the Halt so trains bound for Caerphilly had to be propelled 'wrong line' to Glyntaff Halt, just over half a mile away, where the train could be crossed onto the correct line.

BARRY RAILWAY

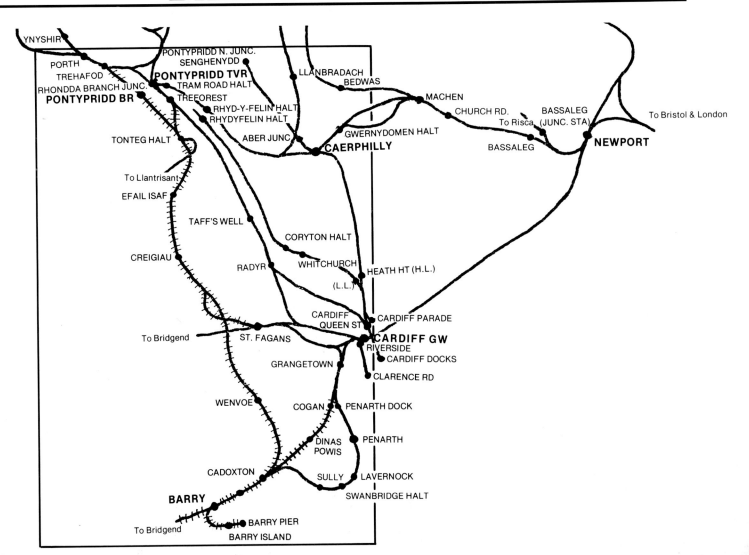

YNYSHIR
PORTH
TREHAFOD
RHONDDA BRANCH JUNC.
PONTYPRIDD BR
PONTYPRIDD N. JUNC.
SENGHENYDD
PONTYPRIDD TVR
TRAM ROAD HALT
TREFOREST
RHYD-Y-FELIN HALT
RHYDYFELIN HALT
TONTEG HALT
ABER JUNC.
LLANBRADACH
BEDWAS
MACHEN
CHURCH RD.
To Risca
BASSALEG
(JUNC. STA)
To Bristol & London
GWERNYDOMEN HALT
CAERPHILLY
BASSALEG
NEWPORT
To Llantrisant
EFAIL ISAF
TAFF'S WELL
CORYTON HALT
CREIGIAU
RADYR
WHITCHURCH
HEATH HT (H.L.)
(L.L.)
CARDIFF
QUEEN ST
CARDIFF PARADE
To Bridgend
ST. FAGANS
CARDIFF GW
RIVERSIDE
CARDIFF DOCKS
GRANGETOWN
CLARENCE RD
WENVOE
COGAN
PENARTH DOCK
DINAS
POWIS
PENARTH
CADOXTON
SULLY
LAVERNOCK
BARRY
SWANBRIDGE HALT
To Bridgend
BARRY PIER
BARRY ISLAND

3 BARRY PIER STATION

This station was at the end of the 43 chain extension from Barry Island Station and was opened in 1899 by the Barry Railway who were trying to further exploit the tourist traffic which had proved so successful at Barry Island, three years earlier. Up until the Barry Railway purchased their own paddle steamers in 1905—the GWALIA, WESTONIA, DEVONIA and BARRY—the firm of P & A Campbell called at Barry Pier with their steamers and after the Barry sold their fleet in 1910 the original arrangement was reverted to. The photograph was taken from the walkway that connected both platforms, looking towards Barry Island Station. Both platforms were used for arrivals and departures with trains allowed to run 'wrong line' between Barry Pier Signalbox and Barry Island Signalbox; the former box can just be seen behind the steps on the left of the footbridge. Of the three somersault signals in view, only two relate to the railway, the one on the left was used for controlling steamers coming alongside the jetty which was situated behind the wall on the left hand platform. It can be seen that the station is lit by electricity as were a lot of other railway premises in the docks' area, power being supplied from the North Power House situated at the North Western corner of No. 1 Dock. The mouth of the 280 yard long tunnel leading to Barry Island is behind the footbridge on the left, while to the right of centre of the same bridge can be seen the mouth of the unlined tunnel through which maintenance trains for the Western Breakwater passed, temporary track being laid across the top of the main line. Four Saxby & Farmer revolving ground discs are shown, three being of the compound variety.

4 BARRY ISLAND STATION

Viewed looking towards Barry with a Barry Railway J Class 2-4-2T and rake of six wheeled carriages stood at Platform 1 forming a train for Cardiff Clarence Road. Platform 1 was extended, to the rear of the photographer, in 1914, the extension becoming Platform 2 and used for excursion traffic. *This* was a siding, operated by a set of points on the Barry Pier side of the crossover in the foreground, leaving Platforms 1 and 3 free to deal with other traffic. The crossover mentioned, along with extra signalling, was brought into use on 29/4/18 and the somersault signals on Platform 3 were, from left to right as seen, as follows:— Down Inner Home Signal for trains proceeding into the No. 2 (Excursion) Platform; Down Main Inner Home Signal; for trains proceeding into the Station Yard; the 'Calling On' arm was for trains requiring to draw to the end of the Down (No. 3) Platform. The GWR remodelled this station further by putting in a loop at the rear of Platform 3 which became Platforms 3 and 4 as well as replacing the signalbox, out of sight to the right, with a standard GWR box, most of the signalling was resited at the same time, replacing the former Barry 'somersaults' with GWR 'semaphores' though in a couple of instances, the original Barry 'somersaults' were resited and at least one lasted until the late 1950's. There was at one time a small goods yard here leading off from the Down Main but very little traffic was handled, the only regular in-coming traffic seems to have been manure for the allotment owners at Barry Island!

5 BARRY STATION

Viewed looking towards Barry Docks Station with Barry Railway B1 Class 0-6-2T No. 60 and a rake of 10 six wheeled carriages leaving for the Vale of Glamorgan. It is interesting to note that the signal finials at Barry differ from those shown at Barry Island even though the signalling was supplied by the same firm. Barry Signalbox is partially visible beneath the footbridge, Barry Junction Signalbox being behind the photographer. On the left of the picture are the main station buildings behind which is the Goods Yard, a passenger train is 'setting back' into the bay platform alongside the latter. Part of the Barry Railway Locomotive, Carriage and Wagon Works can be seen behind the Down, or right hand, Platform and on the extreme right is a Barry Railway four wheeled Mineral Brake in the 'van sidings'. From August 2nd until August 7th, 1920, the Royal National Eisteddfod of Wales was held at Barry, this coincided with the August Bank Holiday resulting in many extra trains being laid on to accommodate the crowds that flocked to Barry and Barry Island during this period, without doubt the busiest days were Monday the 2nd and Tuesday the 3rd of August when no fewer than 237 passenger trains were dealt with at Barry Station between 5.20 a.m. and 11.55 p.m., roughly a train every 4½ minutes! Wednesday saw 225 trains, Thursday and Friday 220 while on Saturday there was a mere 159. Three sets of GW coaches and two sets of L & SWR coaches were borrowed to cover some of the workings by the Barry Railway while Taff Vale, Rhymney and Great Western engines and stock worked through to Barry and Barry Island on excursions, even the Barry's four wheeled Workmen's coaches were pressed into service during the week mentioned.

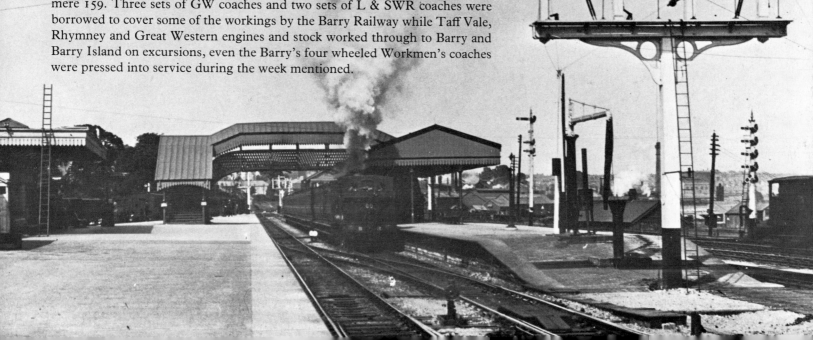

6 BARRY DOCKS STATION

Viewed looking towards Barry Station. A Barry Railway J Class engine, between the Barry Docks Signalbox and the station, is heading for Barry on the Down Main line. The position of Barry Docks Station was originally only temporary, it was intended, at a later date, to re-align the track and move the station to the level ground on the right of the picture, but this work was never carried out. Many complaints were received concerning bad access to the station which was by path and subway, and one person was killed as he walked through the subway on his way to work at the Docks, a loaded platform trolley careered down the approach ramp and into the subway, crushing the victim against the subway wall. There were originally two signalboxes at Barry Docks Station, one at either end of the island platform, the one shown on the right hand side of the picture was, up until the end of 1912, only opened for the busy summer passenger service, at the end of that year a double crossover was put in to the west of the cabin to allow mineral trains on the Up Main line to enter the High Level Sidings instead of having to go to Cadoxton for access into the above mentioned sidings, and it was after this work had been completed that the cabin was brought into 24 hour use. To the left of the picture are a couple of private owner wagons belonging to the Meiros Colliery which was just to the north of Llanharan, they reached Barry Docks via the GWR to Peterston Junction and down the Barry Main Line. The two small huts on the platform in the foreground were for the use of coal-trimmers and were erected in 1913 after complaints of the trimmers using the ordinary waiting room in their working clothes had been received, again, it can be seen that this station is lit by electricity. The refreshment rooms here, which consisted of public bar and lounge bar always did a brisk trade and were leased by Mr. R. P. Culley who ran several hostelries in South Wales including the Barry Dock Hotel which was situated directly opposite the approach to this station.

7 CADOXTON STATION

Viewed looking towards Dinas Powis with the Barry Main Line bearing off to the left at the end of the station and the Cardiff Branch to the right, Cadoxton Station Signalbox can be seen at the end of the platform. Cadoxton Goods Depot is below the signal gantry on the Up platform and the sign to the left of this reads, "Passengers must cross the line by the subway for Platforms 3 & 4.", these latter platforms were used by the Taff Vale Railway for their service to Cardiff via Penarth. Interesting to compare the two different styles of lamps used on the Barry Railway platforms and the Taff Vale Railway platform, in later years, when the station had electricity put in, five of the gas lamps were removed to the steamer jetty at Barry Pier and converted to electricity. Mineral traffic through this station was very heavy and delays in moving the traffic from Cadoxton Sidings to the Docks for shipment were regular as the traffic had to cross the Cardiff Branch with its intensive passenger service so, an Act of Parliament was granted to the Barry Railway in 1897 to allow them to take their mineral lines over the top of Cadoxton Station on flyovers but the work was never carried out and the Act was abandoned in 1927 by the GWR. Another scheme was put forward in 1909 whereby the station was to be put under the mineral lines but it was thought that with gradients of 1 in 65 some of the smaller passenger engines would find difficulty with their trains and so Cadoxton remained a bottleneck. It is difficult to make out the two engines in the yard but the one on the left appears to be Barry Railway H Class No. 85. An interesting note is that as and from midnight Monday the 6th of February, 1922, all the distant signals between Cadoxton Junction and Tynycaeau North, and on the Peterston and St. Fagans branches had their spectacles changed from red to orange glasses and the arms repainted from red and white to orange and black.

8 COGAN STATION

Viewed looking towards Barry, Cogan Signalbox in the centre of the picture. At the rear of the Up, or right hand, platform were a pair of sidings where traffic between the Taff Vale Railway and the Barry Railway was exchanged though the innermost of the two lines was to be kept as clear as possible for the passage of more important trains. The wagons behind the signalbox are in the small goods yard which at one time had its own Goods Shed but nothing of any significant size would be needed here as the Taff Vale Railway had been serving the area for some 25 years before the Barry Railway arrived on the scene. Connection between the two platforms was via a footbridge situated behind the photographer, as is the path that led from Cogan Station to the Taff Vale Railway station at Penarth Dock, some 100 yards away, this path would have been used quite considerably by passengers from Barry to Cardiff between 1888 and 1893 for the Barry Railway opened their branch to Cogan on the 20th December, 1888 but were not granted running powers into Cardiff Riverside until the 14th August, 1893 so passengers for Cardiff had to change trains at Cogan.

9 COGAN STATION

Again looking towards Barry but with the Swansea-Newcastle 'Ports to Ports' express passing through behind a GWR 'Bulldog' 4-4-0, GW and GC stock was used on alternate days. This service originally ran from Newcastle to Cardiff but was extended to Barry on the 1st August, 1906, a Barry Railway engine taking over from the GW engine at Cardiff for the remainder of the journey to Barry. From Monday the 12th July, 1920, the train was further extended to Swansea which resulted in GW engines working the train west of Cardiff as seen here. Until the GW enginemen got to know the road the Barry Railway supplied Pilot Drivers and Pilot Guards for the train which was later re-routed to take in Penarth and rejoined the Barry Railway at Biglis Junction. It is very unfortunate that this photograph is blurred which spoils a fairly rare shot of the express at Cogan where speed through the station and junction would be no more than 8 miles per hour.

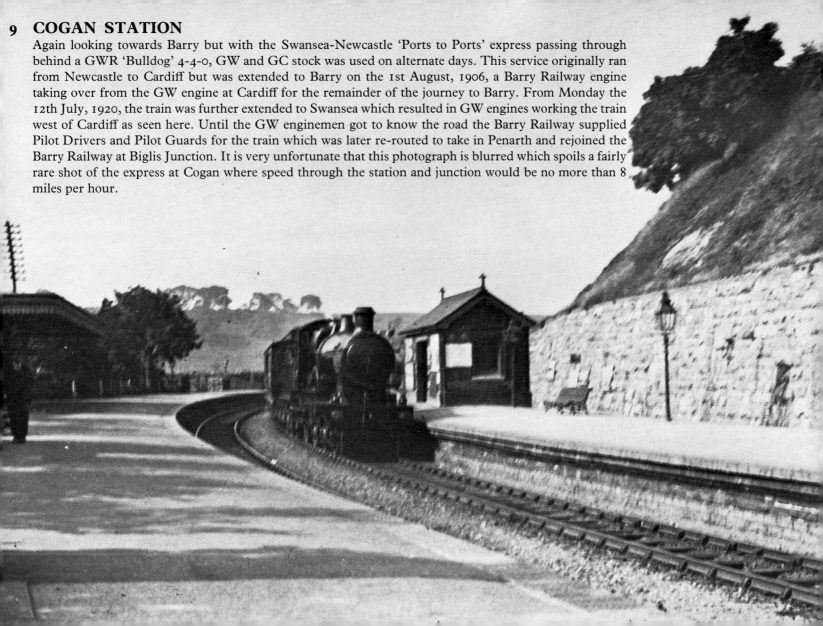

PASSENGERS
MUST CROSS
THE LINE BY
THE BRIDGE

10 CREIGIAU STATION

Viewed looking towards Barry. Unlike the Cardiff Branch of the Barry Railway, the main line northward from Cadoxton had some quite severe gradients though in most cases they were with the train. Creigiau Signalbox was situated at the other side of the road bridge on the Up, or right hand, side, there was also a ground frame on the south end of the Down Relief line, again all Saxby & Farmer signalling from the revolving ground discs to the essentially tall somersault signals for sighting purposes. The signal at the south end of the Up platform is of extreme interest as it dates the print fairly accurately to June, 1921, this was the setting back signal from the Up main into the Up siding and as can be seen is not yet in use but, the signal was brought into use on Monday the 4th July, 1921. The type of footbridge seen here at Creigiau is of the standard type used on the Barry system though at some stations, such as Barry, they were enclosed. Approaching the station is what appears to be a Barry Railway B Class 0-6-2T with a train of mineral empties but again, due to camera shake, this cannot be taken as definite.

11 CREIGIAU STATION

Viewed looking towards Efail Isaf and showing the rather ornate footbridge, complete with gas lamps, in full. The main station building on the Down side with a twin gable roof is the same as those that were at Efail Isaf and Wenvoe, though the upright from the horizontal beam of the barge boards to the apex of the roof is partly obscured by the gas lamp on the footbridge. Between the last two gas lamps on the Down platform it is just possible to discern the track of the Taff Vale's Waterhall Junction-Common Branch Junction line, although both Companies' lines were so close to each other no connection was made between the two except during the construction of the Barry Main Line when a single line was laid from about the end of the platforms to just beyond the road overbridge in the distance where it connected with the Taff Vale line and was used for bringing in construction equipment and material. This line was 462 yards in length and known on the Barry Contract as Railway No. 6.

12 PONTYPRIDD STATION (BARRY RAILWAY)

Viewed looking south towards Treforest, the 1,323 yard long Pontypridd Tunnel is seen at the end of the platforms, in later years subsidence due to mining activity became a major problem within the tunnel. Worthy of note is the decorative ironwork on the outside and beneath the station canopy on the Down platform, also the use of suspended gas lamps. The small hut between the station canopy on the Down platform and the road bridge was Pontypridd Station Ground Frame but it was taken out of use on Monday the 14th February, 1921, along with the Up Home Signal which was situated on the Up platform, just north of the tunnel mouth.

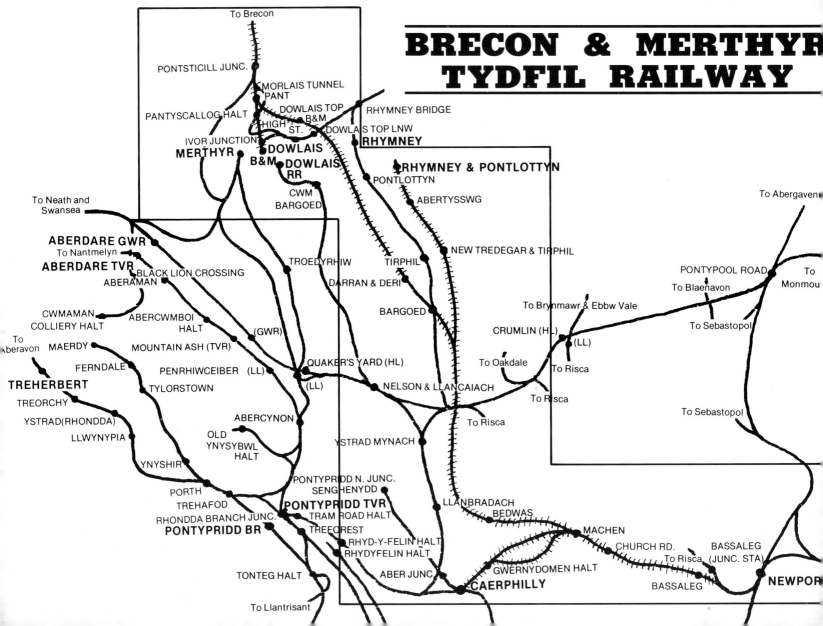

BRECON & MERTHYR TYDFIL RAILWAY

13 MACHEN STATION

Viewed looking west from the Up platform with the 11.20 a.m. ex Rhymney-Newport train arriving behind B&M 4-4-2T No. 44, which, at this time, was the oldest engine belonging to this Company and the only one of this wheel arrangement, this engine of LSWR origin was acquired by the B&M in 1914 and scrapped by the GWR in November, 1922. It is rather unfortunate that when the photographer managed to capture an engine and train with his camera, it resulted in slight blurring in several cases, as shown here for example.

14 MACHEN STATION

Again viewed looking west towards Bedwas with Machen Junction in the background, where the line for Caerphilly went off to the left and the main line hugged the side of the valley as it continued westward to Bedwas before turning north for Rhymney. The line to Caerphilly was somewhat unusual in that the Up and Down lines were separated for part of their route in order that easier gradients could be followed before the lines came together again east of Gwernydomen Halt. Like a lot of other stations in South Wales, Machen was reached by a steep hill from the town below. In the bay alongside the Up platform are three wagons of the Tredegar Navigation Colliery and an unidentified five plank wagon whilst at the far end of the Down platform stands Machen Signalbox; a little further on, on the Down side, was the three levered ground frame for working the Machen Station North Siding. Signalling on the Brecon & Merthyr was supplied by McKenzie & Holland and a good example of their work can be seen in this photograph along with their very distinctive style of finial. The main station building on the Up platform looks rather depressing with its cement-rendered walls and yet the smaller stations of Rhiwderin and Church Road had very attractive buildings, both of which are now in private ownership. At the junction for the Caerphilly line is the former No. 2 Rail-motor of the ADR, by now converted to an ordinary carriage.

15 NEW TREDEGAR & TIRPHIL STATION

Viewed looking south towards Pengam (Mon.), with New Tredegar Goods Shed in the middle distance which is a variant of the B&M's usual ridge roofed pattern, but still with the apex of the end walls filled with glazing. This section of the line north of Pengam being known as the Rhymney Branch of the B&M. The Barry Railway paid for the doubling of the track from Duffryn Isaf to Abertysswg, and the up-grading of certain sections of single line as well as extra signals and signalboxes to enable the Barry Company to reach Rhymney but, to join the B&M at Duffryn Isaf, it was necessary for the Barry Railway to construct Llanbradach Viaduct and the traffic that came over this route between its opening in 1905 and the Grouping never warranted such an expensive venture, it being very doubtful if the Barry had broken even by 1922. The B&M were not worried though, they had had a first class main line built for them and even made the Barry Company put in its own water supply at Whiterose, claiming that they, the B&M, only had enough water for their own engines but, they felt sure that if B&M engines did need water, the Barry wouldn't mind them using their supply at Whiterose! Such was the way of the B&M, cheeky but extremely resourceful. A landslip to the north of New Tredegar & Tirphil Station in 1930 closed the section of track to Rhymney.

16 ABERTYSSWG STATION

Viewed looking south towards New Tredegar with the McLaren No. 1 Colliery in the background and the colliers' platform serving the same to the right of the picture, with a colliers' train, which includes some former LSWR four wheeled carriages, in the siding at the rear of the platform. From here to Rhymney the line was single and worked by Electric Train Tablet, the double line ending near McLaren No. 1 Colliery. From Aberbargoed to Rhymney the line was on a steady rising gradient of 1 in 98 for the $5\frac{3}{4}$ miles and with curves such as here at Abertysswg, it must have been a tricky job starting away with Rhymney bound trains.

17 RHYMNEY & PONTLOTTYN STATION

This station is viewed towards the end of the branch with the derelict McClaren No. 2 Colliery to the rear of the station. The line continued past the station, across the Mardy Level Crossing and into the Rhymney Iron Company's Works which were off to the left of the photograph and by this time closed, sidings also led into the McClaren No. 2 Colliery. The station was renamed by the GWR on two occasions, firstly to Rhymney (Pwll Uchaf) and two years later it became Rhymney (Lower). Of interest is the B&M Iron Mink No. 500 on the extreme right of the picture, which, as can be plainly seen, is vacuum fitted, a fact not recorded in the GWR Wagon Register, in which the van is renumbered GW101558.

18 DOWLAIS TOP STATION and JUNCTION

Viewed looking towards Pant with the LNWR coming in from the left foreground with a branch off their Abergavenny-Dowlais line to join the B&M main line, one of the more inhospitable B&M locations. The Abergavenny-Dowlais line was at a lower level than the B&M and a semaphore signal on the former line can just be seen near the telegraph pole on the left of the picture. The B&M line from Fochriw to Dowlais Top was not that dissimilar to a switchback with gradients of 1 in 100/40 and 38 falling towards Fochriw and 1 in 50 and 73 falling towards Dowlais Top, after which the line continued at 1 in 56/105 and 60 falling towards Pant, in fact, as the line curves out of the station towards Pant it can be seen to drop away. It is hardly surprising that B&M enginemen who were used to working trains over such tortuous routes never experienced any difficulty in finding work with some of the better paying South Wales railway companies. If they could work trains on the B&M, they could work them anywhere!

19 IVOR JUNCTION

Viewed looking towards Pant with the B&M line from Dowlais to the former in the left foreground and the LNWR line from Dowlais High Street Station coming in from the right. On the extreme right is the private line of the Dowlais Iron Co., which was taken over by Guest Keen & Co. in 1901, this title changed to the more familiar Guest, Keen & Nettlefolds the following year. The line cutting right across that of the B&M is again that of GKN and it was known as the Cinder Tip Road, which led out to near Bryniau where there were tips for that purpose. Arguably the most interesting feature in the photograph concerns the derelict buildings to the right of the signalbox for this was the former LNWR engine shed at Dowlais. It was built by the LNWR in 1871 for their passenger engines that were employed on the Dowlais Top (LNWR)-Dowlais B&M service, but this ceased when the LNWR built their own station at Dowlais High Street and the shed fell into disuse. In 1887 the B&M shed at Pant caught fire and the Company rented the engine shed at Ivor Junction from the LNWR until the B&M built and opened an engine shed at Dowlais B&M in 1898, after which, the shed at Ivor Junction again fell into disuse.

Viewed looking in the same direction as the previous photograph but showing the large B&M signal gantry and on the right, an 0-4-0 outside cylinder, cabless, saddle tank under the ownership of Guest, Keen & Nettlefolds. Whether this engine is going to couple up to the string of bolster wagons or has been, or is going to the Cinder Tip isn't known, but whichever it is, she's got a good head of steam ready! The WHISTLE board to the left of the signalbox was for the protection of the Hafod Road Crossing which enginemen were warned "to approach with great caution". The line from Pant to the far side of Ivor Junction Signalbox was single but from there to Dowlais No. 1 Signalbox the line was double, it being only 21 chains from the former to the end of the branch which, for most of its length, was on a falling gradient towards Pant with the ruling sections being 1 in 56/105 and 60.

21 DOWLAIS STATION B & M

Viewed looking towards Ivor Junction with a train for Pant stood at the platform, the cattle dock being to the right of the train. From Dowlais No. 1 Signalbox to the station the track was of two single lines, the passenger line being used for Up and Down traffic and the goods line, next to it, being used in the same manner, carrying on past the station to the large goods shed situated to the rear of the photographer. The building on the left of the photograph is the engine shed of 1916 vintage, the shed of 1898 mentioned earlier being destroyed by a blizzard in March, 1916. The MR wagons alongside the shed probably came onto the B&M metals at Talyllyn Junction.

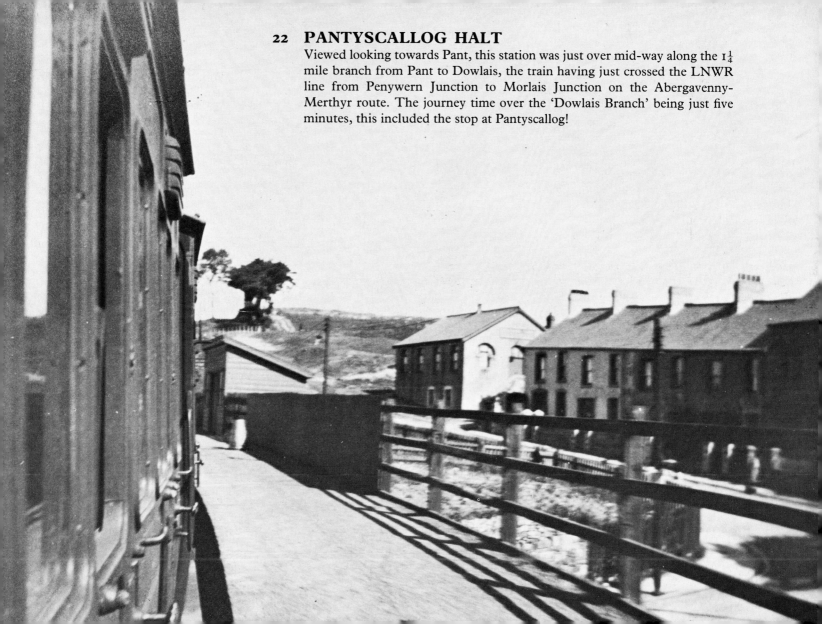

22 PANTYSCALLOG HALT

Viewed looking towards Pant, this station was just over mid-way along the $1\frac{1}{4}$ mile branch from Pant to Dowlais, the train having just crossed the LNWR line from Penywern Junction to Morlais Junction on the Abergavenny-Merthyr route. The journey time over the 'Dowlais Branch' being just five minutes, this included the stop at Pantyscallog!

23 PANT STATION

Viewed looking northwards towards Pontsticill, and what a lovely rural scene it looks as well, a far cry from the bleak and desolate scene it could present in the depths of the winter months. The train in the middle distance is coming off the Dowlais Branch to join the B&M main line at Pant Junction, some 9 chains outside the station, before setting back into the Up, or left hand, platform. The platform for Dowlais Branch trains was at the rear of the Up platform, but at a lower level, a set of steps connected the two. Back to the main line station, it can be seen that passengers who wanted to catch a down train crossed the track just beyond the signalbox, only a pair of 'Beware of Trains' notices protecting their safety. Above the train on the Dowlais Branch, on the skyline, can be seen the tops of several mineral wagons, these are on the internal track of Morlais Quarries which connected up with the B&M's Dowlais Branch south of Pant Station.

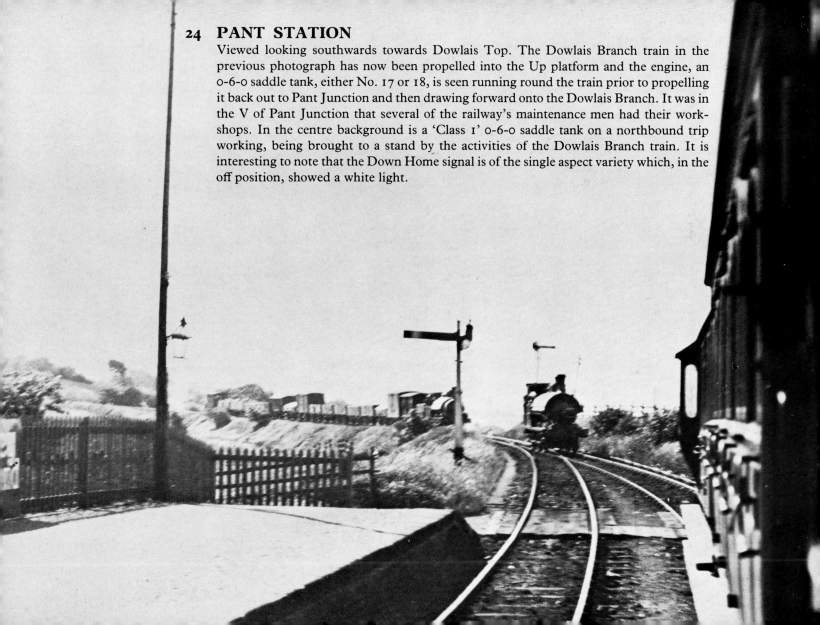

24 PANT STATION

Viewed looking southwards towards Dowlais Top. The Dowlais Branch train in the previous photograph has now been propelled into the Up platform and the engine, an 0-6-0 saddle tank, either No. 17 or 18, is seen running round the train prior to propelling it back out to Pant Junction and then drawing forward onto the Dowlais Branch. It was in the V of Pant Junction that several of the railway's maintenance men had their workshops. In the centre background is a 'Class 1' 0-6-0 saddle tank on a northbound trip working, being brought to a stand by the activities of the Dowlais Branch train. It is interesting to note that the Down Home signal is of the single aspect variety which, in the off position, showed a white light.

25 PONTSTICILL JUNCTION STATION

Viewed looking north towards Brecon showing the original B&M footbridge which a GWR Steam Crane later demolished by passing under it with its jib up! The photograph was taken from the actual junction with the Merthyr lines seen to be joining those of the main line from Pant in the foreground. In the yard to the left of the station stands a goods train for the Merthyr Branch behind one of the B&M's double framed 0-6-0 saddle tanks, note the rolled up tarpaulin on the spartan cab roof, no point in taking chances in this area where the weather can change by the minute!

26 MORLAIS TUNNEL

The western portal of the LNWR's 1,040 yard long Morlais Tunnel that passed under both the B&M's Dowlais Branch and Main Line, as seen from a B&M Pontsticill Junction-Merthyr train which is just crossing Morlais Junction. The line from here to Merthyr was B&M/LNWR Joint, Morlais Junction Signalbox being an LNWR structure working B&M signalling on the B&M side and Crewe pressed steel pattern signals on the LNWR side, the LNWR also supplied Webb & Thompson staffs for the Morlais Junction-Rhydycar Junction section of the line.

CARDIFF RAILWAY

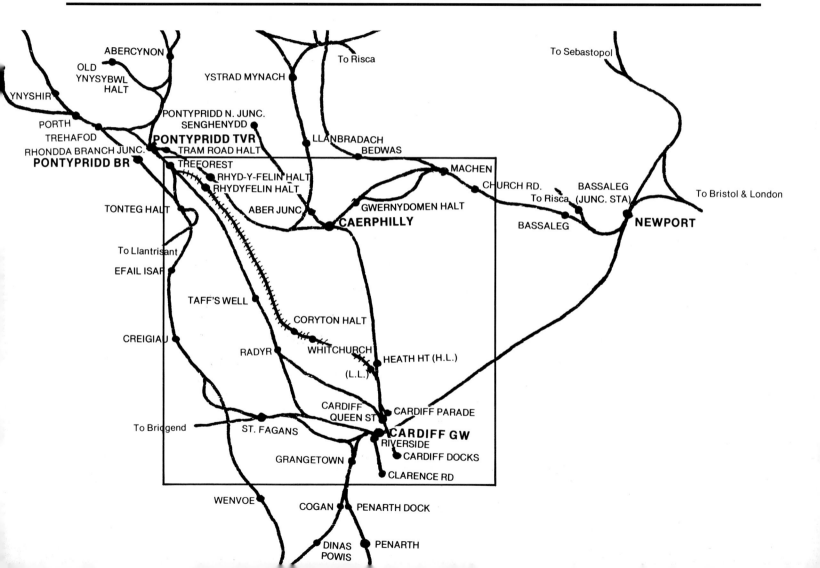

27 WHITCHURCH STATION

Viewed looking east towards Rhiwbina Halt, the footbridge of which can just be made out in the distance. The station buildings are typical of the larger type built by the Cardiff Railway though at Glanllyn the station's name was displayed on the front of the station canopy. The Cardiff Railway was promoted with a view of running from a junction with the TVR at Treforest to Heath Junction where the Rhymney Railway had granted the CR running powers onto its own dock railway network but the problem was that the Cardiff Railway had specified that the junction was to be made with the TVR's passenger line which, at Treforest, was geographically impossible. So, the line was opened for passenger traffic only as far as Rhydyfelin Halt. Judging by the amount of grass and stubble growing on the platform faces at Whitchurch it suggests that passenger figures were none too high at this time but, as Cardiff developed all the surrounding land was used for the construction of housing and the railway became an important inner suburban line, albeit in its truncated form from Coryton to Heath Junction. As can be seen from the size of the Goods Shed and yard, the Cardiff Railway envisaged a certain amount of goods traffic to originate from within the area served by the railway.

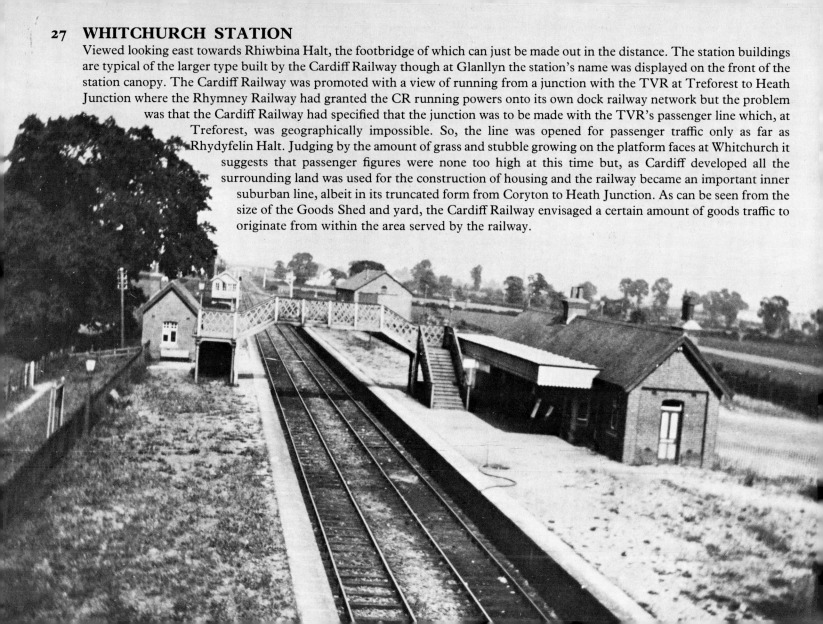

28 RHYDYFELIN HALT

Terminus of the Cardiff Railway passenger service and viewed looking south towards Upper Boat. This was a rail level halt, the double line continuing for approximately a further one third of a mile before coming to an abrupt end on an embankment in the middle of a field! This was due to the difficulties already mentioned with the Taff Vale Railway. There were a pair of crossovers at Rhydyfelin which not only allowed the steam railmotors to go from the Down to Up lines, but also allowed for engines to run round a train of carriages. Signalling was by McKenzie & Holland and the small building next to the water column is a coal stage for the use of the steam railmotors that had quite a limited coal carrying capacity. In the background, just below the eaves of the coal stage can be seen the line of the Alexandra Docks & Railway Co's route from Penrhos Junction to Pontypridd Tram Road Halt.

GREAT WESTERN RAILWAY

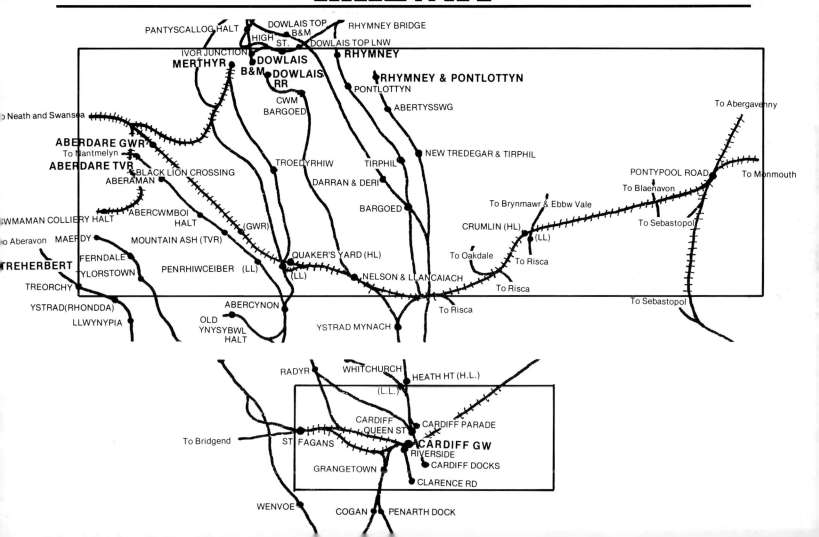

29 CARDIFF CLARENCE ROAD STATION

Viewed looking towards the end of the Riverside Branch which the GWR originally only used for goods traffic. By an agreement with the Taff Vale Railway, Barry Railway and Great Western Railway, the former two Companies were allowed to run passenger trains from Clarence Road, the Barry Railway were also allowed to use the branch for goods traffic but seldom exercised this right. Taff Vale trains using the station would be for Penarth and Cadoxton whilst those of the Barry Railway were for Barry and Pontypridd via St. Fagans and Tynycaeau Junction. The Riverside Branch was only 70 chains in length, double track throughout but with only one platform at Clarence Road, on the west side of the line. In the platform is a Taff Vale train for Penarth, note the destination boards under the carriage windows.

30 CARDIFF CLARENCE ROAD STATION

Viewed looking in the same direction as the previous photograph with the same train stood at the platform behind Taff Vale Railway 'A' Class No. 410, if the date of June, 1921 is correct for these photographs, the engine was taken into TVR stock only five months previous, being built by Hawthorn, Leslie & Co. Clarence Road Station Signalbox was to the right and rear of the photographer.

31 CARDIFF RIVERSIDE STATION

Viewed looking westwards towards Penarth Junction, this station adjoined Cardiff G.W. and later became Platforms 8 and 9 of that station. Riverside Station was the scene of what could have been a very bad accident in the afternoon of the 23/2/23, when a train for Barry, standing in the Down platform and containing some 500 passengers, was run into by a Clarence Road to Pontypridd train, derailing and slightly telescoping the rear two carriages of the Barry train. This accident resulted in only 31 injuries, 28 of them slight, the cause of the accident being attributed to signalman error at Cardiff West Signalbox which is just visible in the middle background of the photograph. The Board of Trade Inspecting Officer, Colonel Mount, was surprised "in that there existed at Riverside Station no supplementary means, for example, track circuiting with the usual locking, of reminding the signalman in the West Box of trains standing within his control."

32 CARDIFF RIVERSIDE STATION

Again, viewed looking westward towards Penarth Junction, the signalbox for which is just left of centre. The Riverside Branch lines being the two to the left of the photographer, those on the far left were the carriage sidings at the rear of Riverside Station, the sidings in the foreground, behind the two men, were known as the Fish Jetty Dock. On the right of the picture is the short lived baggage hoist that spanned all the through lines, while on the left the semaphore signal is quite interesting with what appears to be the letters Bch (Branch) on the Home Arm but those on the arm of the Fixed Distant, apart from TV, are not clear enough to be read.

33 CARDIFF GW STATION

Again viewed looking west towards Penarth Junction from the end of Platform 3, the bay Platform 5 being to the left. Cardiff West Signalbox is behind the baggage lift which was mentioned previously, the lines from left to right of centre are Down passenger, Down relief, Up relief and Up passenger. To the right of the photograph, in the small goods yard, a horse is shunting vans in the sidings. Of interest is the painting date on the baggage lift which is 4 22, so presumably, the photographer paid two visits to South Wales, one in 1921 which is clarified by the photographs of Creigiau and Pontypridd BR, and again in 1922 where it looks as though he might have concentrated his efforts more on the main line.

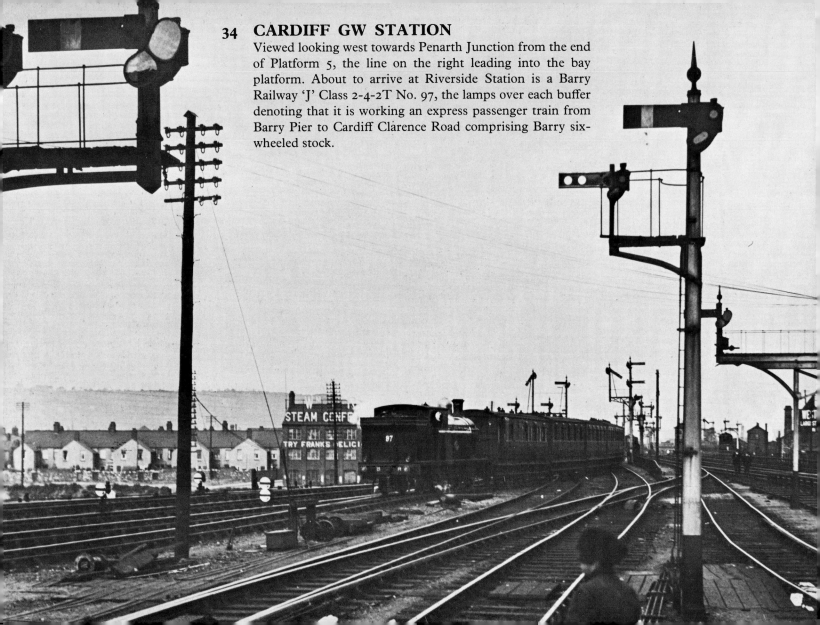

34 CARDIFF GW STATION

Viewed looking west towards Penarth Junction from the end of Platform 5, the line on the right leading into the bay platform. About to arrive at Riverside Station is a Barry Railway 'J' Class 2-4-2T No. 97, the lamps over each buffer denoting that it is working an express passenger train from Barry Pier to Cardiff Clarence Road comprising Barry six-wheeled stock.

35 CARDIFF GW STATION

Viewed looking east towards Newport with a Taff Vale 'A' Class 0-6-2T coming down the bank from Cardiff Queen Street Station, the train will be going into Platform 6. The photograph was taken from the east end of Platform 3, those that know this Cardiff station today may be excused for not recognising the location immediately! The lines from left to right are as follows, on the very far side next to the brake van is the line for the bay Platform 2, Up passenger, Up relief, Down relief, Down passenger, Up line for Queen Street and Down line from same, Cardiff East Signalbox is adjacent to the latter.

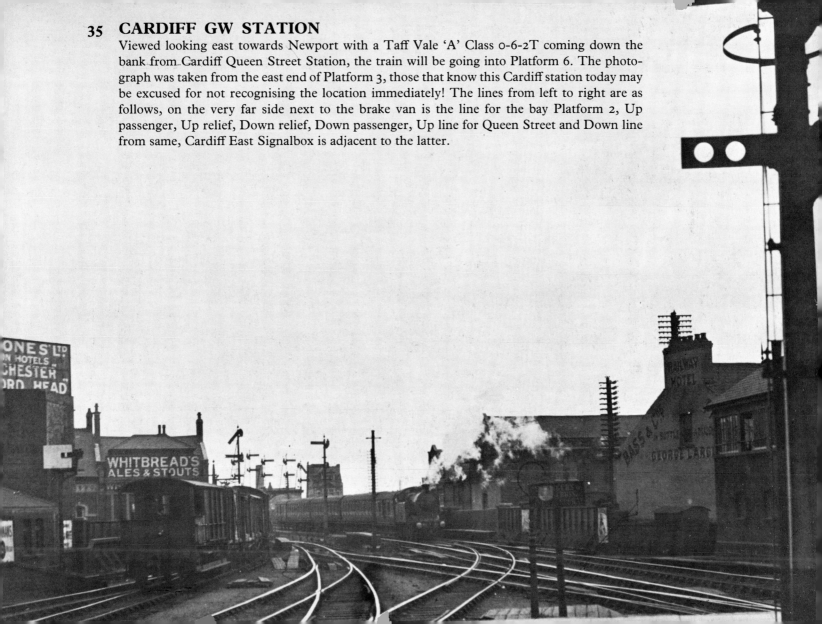

36 PONTYPOOL ROAD STATION

Viewed looking north towards Hereford with what appears to be a '517' Class 0-4-2 tank on the Up relief line, Pontypool Road did not have any '517' Class engines allocated to it at the time so the engine may have worked in from Pontrilas or Ross-on-Wye, there being a bay at the northern end of this island platform station, the bay on the south end of the station, on the right of the picture with empty stock stabled in it, was usually used by trains on the Pontypool Road-Neath, via Aberdare, service. Entrance to the platforms was by subway from the station approach road.

37 PONTYPOOL ROAD STATION

Viewed looking south towards Newport, the main station buildings are to the left of the running lines behind which can be seen the station approach road mentioned previously. Just beyond the road bridge in the centre background was the site of the original station at Pontypool. Pontypool Road was quite a busy railway centre, with lines radiating to places such as Newport, Aberdare, Cwmffrwd, Brynmawr, Abergavenny and Monmouth and at this time the number of engines allocated to the depot at Pontypool Road exceeded eighty.

38 QUAKERS YARD (HIGH LEVEL) STATION

Viewed looking north-easterly towards Mountain Ash, the line joining the main line at the end of the right hand platform was that of the Great Western & Rhymney Joint line to Merthyr. The Taff Vale station that the name board applies to was at a lower level to the left of this photograph, the footbridge serving both stations. Quakers Yard High Level was on the Pontypool Road-Aberdare line, it being sixteen miles from the former station, there was a connection with the Taff Vale's low level station by means of a line a half a mile to the east of Quakers Yard HL Station, the connection being 41 chains in length.

39 MERTHYR STATION

This terminus is viewed from the south with a train for Pontsticill Junction leaving behind a B&M saddle tank while on the right, on the RR/GWR Joint Line stands a RR engine and train for Cardiff, apart from these two companies, the station was used by the TVR, the Cambrian in the summer months, the L&NWR and, of course, the GWR. What a sight it must have been to see the engines and stock of these various companies working in and out of this station that was originally the broad gauge terminus of the Vale of Neath Railway and constructed by none other than the renowned I. K. Brunel who left his unmistakable stamp on the design of the train shed.

40 MOUNTAIN ASH (CARDIFF ROAD) STATION

Viewed looking south towards Quakers Yard HL which is three miles distant. On the far right of the picture is the Taff Vale Railway's Abercynon-Aberdare line which was in direct opposition to the GW line, both Companies serving Aberdare via the same valley but on opposite sides, a very typical practice within South Wales. The collieries from left to right are Nixon's North Pit which was built as a coal producing pit but used as an upcast shaft for Nixon's Navigation which is the pit to the right, and Deep Duffryn which is behind the photographer. The colliery in the distance, beneath the headgear of Nixon's Navigation is Nixon's Abergorki Colliery.

41 ABERDARE (HIGH LEVEL) STATION

Viewed looking in a north westerly direction towards Neath, Gadlys Junction, where the Taff Vale line made a connection with the GWR line being 30 chains distant. The GWR Goods Shed on the Up side was originally the Vale of Neath Railway terminus at Aberdare, note also the staggered platforms, this was due to close proximity of the Afon Cynon on the Down side of the line, the river passed under the railway at the far end of the Up platform. In the background is the Aberdare High Level Yard Signalbox, there were several sidings on the Down side but the main yard and engine shed were on the Up side behind the station and goods shed. The station approach road is between the railway and the goods shed, the booking office being inside the building at the top of the road.

42 BLACK LION CROSSING HALT

Viewed looking in a south westerly direction towards Cwmaman, a typical GWR branch line halt in an industrial environment. The branch from Gelli Tarw Junction to Cwmaman was laid originally for mineral traffic but in 1906 a motor train service was introduced between Black Lion Crossing and Cwmaman, a distance of 2¾ miles, this service ceased in 1924. To work the branch, the GWR allocated two steam railmotors to their shed at Aberdare and in 1921 Nos. 50 and 51 were used on the branch service.

43 CWMAMAN COLLIERY HALT

Viewed looking in an easterly direction towards Black Lion Crossing with a steam railmotor stood at the platform waiting to work back to the latter. There were also four other halts on the branch apart from the main two already mentioned and these were Ton Llwyd, Godreaman, Cwmneol and Cwmaman Crossing, the journey time from Black Lion Crossing to Cwmaman being 15 minutes. The colliery in the right background is Bedlwyn Cwmaman, Cwmaman Colliery being behind the photographer.

44 CWMAMAN COLLIERY

The end of the GWR branch from Gelli Tarw Junction as seen from the end of Cwmaman Colliery Halt, note the colliers' train to the right of the photograph, also the sheep grazing on the track, a scene very common in South Wales even today.

LONDON & NORTH WESTERN RAILWAY

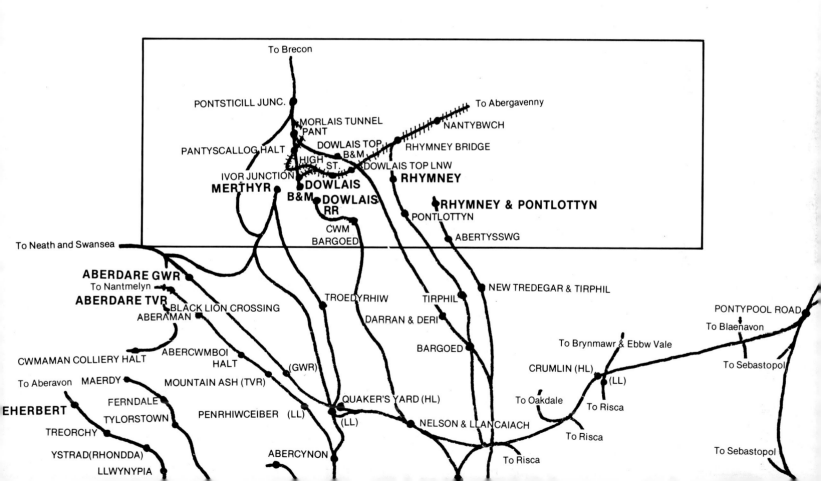

To Brecon

PONTSTICILL JUNC.

MORLAIS TUNNEL
PANT

To Abergavenny

NANTYBWCH

PANTYSCALLOG HALT

DOWLAIS TOP
B&M

RHYMNEY BRIDGE

HIGH ST.

DOWLAIS TOP LNW

IVOR JUNCTION

MERTHYR

DOWLAIS

B&M DOWLAIS
RR

RHYMNEY

RHYMNEY & PONTLOTTYN

PONTLOTTYN

CWM
BARGOED

ABERTYSSWG

To Neath and Swansea

ABERDARE GWR
To Nantmelyn

ABERDARE TVR

BLACK LION CROSSING

ABERAMAN

NEW TREDEGAR & TIRPHIL

TROEDYRHIW

TIRPHIL

PONTYPOOL ROAD

To Blaenavon

DARRAN & DERI

CWMAMAN COLLIERY HALT

ABERCWMBOI
HALT

To Brynmawr & Ebbw Vale

BARGOED

To Aberavon

MAERDY

MOUNTAIN ASH (TVR)

(GWR)

CRUMLIN (HL)

To Sebastopol

FERNDALE

EHERBERT

TYLORSTOWN

TREORCHY

YSTRAD(RHONDDA)

LLWYNYPIA

PENRHIWCEIBER (LL)

ABERCYNON

QUAKER'S YARD (HL)

(LL)

To Oakdale

(LL)

To Risca

NELSON & LLANCAIACH

To Risca

To Risca

To Sebastopol

45 DOWLAIS HIGH STREET STATION

Viewed looking in a north-westerly direction towards Morlais Junction. The LNWR opened this station at Dowlais to offer a better passenger service to the town than had been possible at their other station at Dowlais Top which closed not long after High Street was opened. This station was on the LNWR's Abergavenny to Merthyr route.

46 DOWLAIS TOP STATION

Viewed looking in an easterly direction towards Abergavenny, this was the original LNWR station in the Dowlais area, Dowlais Top Junction being in the foreground. The lines to the left led to the B&M's Dowlais Top Station, 17 chains away, while the lines to the right led down to Cwm Bargoed Junction where one set of lines went to the place of that name and the others to Dowlais High Street. The line seen crossing the LNWR in the background is the B&M's main line from Pant to Deri Junction. It's a pity that the photographer didn't photograph the junction from the B&M line as it would then have been possible to have a better view of the station which, as can be seen, is fenced off from the running line.

RHYMNEY RAILWAY

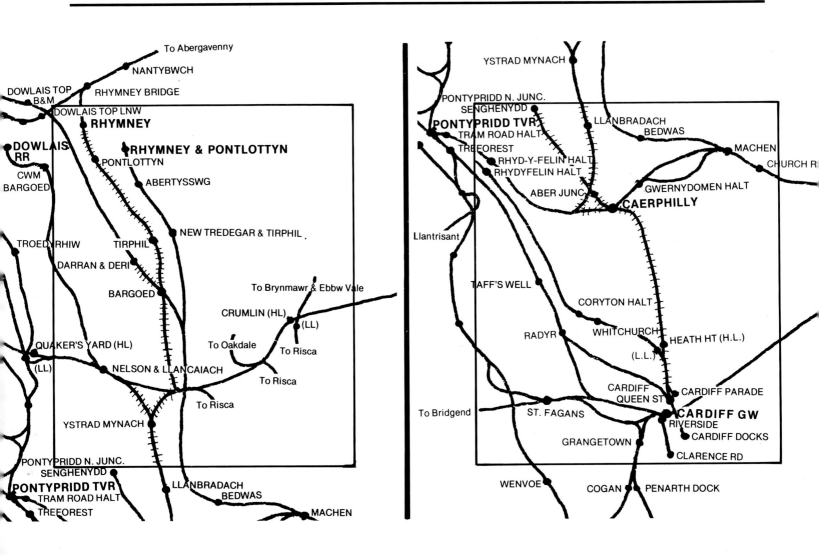

47 PARADE STATION

Showing the exterior of the Rhymney Railway's main passenger station in Cardiff, the original terminus was at Adams Street, 14 chains to the south, but this was converted to goods use and Parade Station was opened, though it was originally called Crockherbtown, after the Cardiff district within which the station lay.

Looking northwards towards Caerphilly from the arrival platform, as can be seen from the station nameboard the Rhymney Railway also called the station Cardiff. To the left of the picture, alongside the TVR somersault signals, is stabled a Cardiff Railway railmotor set, the signalbox which is partly visible to the right of the set is the TVR's Crockherbtown Lower Junction. Parade Station consisted of two through platforms and a bay platform which was the departure platform.

49 PARADE STATION

Looking in a southerly direction and showing the close proximity of the TVR's Queen Street Station, the northern end of which is in the centre background. Parade Station had staggered platforms and this view is taken from the arrival platform, the reason for them being staggered are the lines at the rear of the departure platform, the nearest being the Up mineral line of the Rhymney whilst the outer two are the Up and Down lines that joined the TVR at Crockherbtown Upper Junction. The sign is quite interesting at the end of the platform as it reads:— NOTICE to DRIVERS. Nos. of WAGONS TAKEN HERE. TRAINS go SLOWLY. Note the lamp on the outside of the number taker's cabin, behind the sign, for this purpose.

50 PARADE STATION

Viewed looking south from the departure platform, the arrival platforms can be seen above the carriage roofs to the right of the picture, the signalbox is the Rhymney Railway's Cardiff Station Signalbox. The passenger traffic from this station was quite lucrative as far as the Rhymney Railway was concerned with over 800,000 passengers using the station annually, the Rhymney's Salisbury Road Goods Depot was near here as well, being to the right of the photographer.

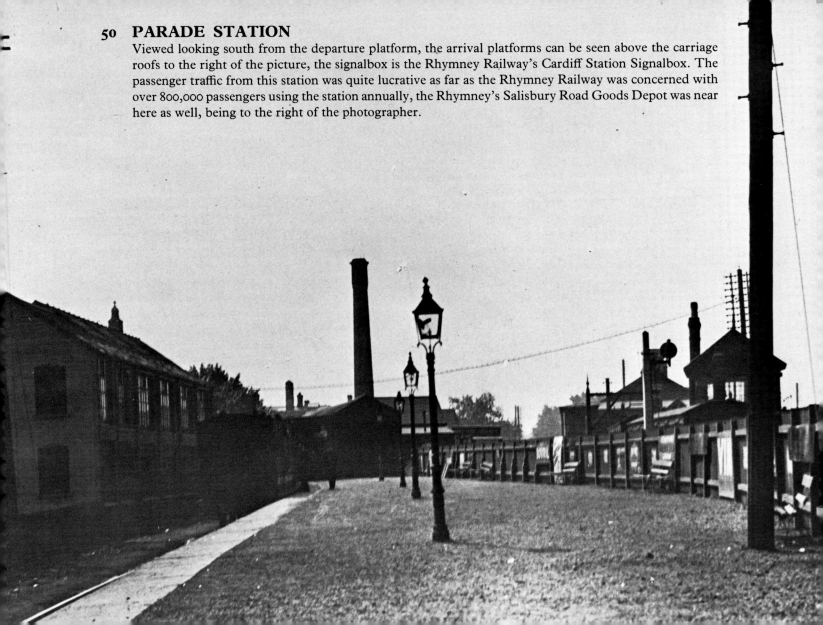

51 CAERPHILLY STATION

Viewed looking south towards Cardiff from the Down platform, the left hand side of which was a bay platform. It must have been very interesting to visit this station some 15 years earlier than when this photograph was taken as it was then possible not only to see Rhymney engines at work but also those of the ADR, GWR (working the Newport-Pontypridd service for the ADR) and B&M. The Rhymney Railway constructed their Locomotive, Carriage and Wagon Works at Caerphilly, these were to the south of the station, on the Down side of the Main line. To the right of the photograph a RR 'A' Class 0-6-2T is passing through the station with a down mineral train.

52 CAERPHILLY STATION

Viewed looking north, again from the Down platform with a RR 'S' Class 0-6-0T in the centre of the photograph, to the right of which can be seen Caerphilly West Signalbox, the main station buildings span the running lines, a typical Rhymney Railway practice which made the station look a bit spartan. On the northern side of Caerphilly West Signalbox was West Branch Junction, the main line to Rhymney bearing to the right and the line to the left led to Watford Crossing Junction, Penrhos Junction and Taffs Well where the Rhymney Railway had a small single road shed, known as Walnut Tree Junction Shed, that housed a pair of banking engines for assisting mineral trains to Penrhos Junction.

53 BARGOED STATION *(Overleaf)*

Viewed looking northwards towards Rhymney with Bargoed North Junction in the background, the Rhymney Railway main line going off to the right and crossing the very imposing Bargoed Viaduct, while the line for Darran & Deri went off to the left, clinging to the hillside for the first part of its route. The B&M made connection with the Rhymney 16 chains to the south of the station at Bargoed South Junction from where they had running powers over the RR, through Bargoed Station and Darran & Deri to rejoin their own line at Deri Junction, in fact, a B&M passenger train can be seen at the platform on the left of the photograph. The Goods Shed is at the rear of the waiting room and parcels office on the Down, or right hand, platform, again, the main station buildings are seen spanning the running lines. On the Down platform it can be seen that one section is lower than the other, this low section is the height of the platform as originally built, the waiting room preventing this section being raised to the height of the adjoining section.

54 DOWLAIS STATION

Viewed looking north, this was the terminus of the RR/Joint Taff-Bargoed Branch from Taff Bargoed Junction, just north of Nelson & Llacaiach. The Goods Depot here was situated near enough to the right of the photographer whilst behind him, and to his left, was the engine shed. The line crossing over the sidings, and disappearing behind the Dowlais Iron Company train stood in the sidings, led to the Dowlais Iron Company's Works, the chimney of which can be seen above the nearest van.

TAFF VALE RAILWAY

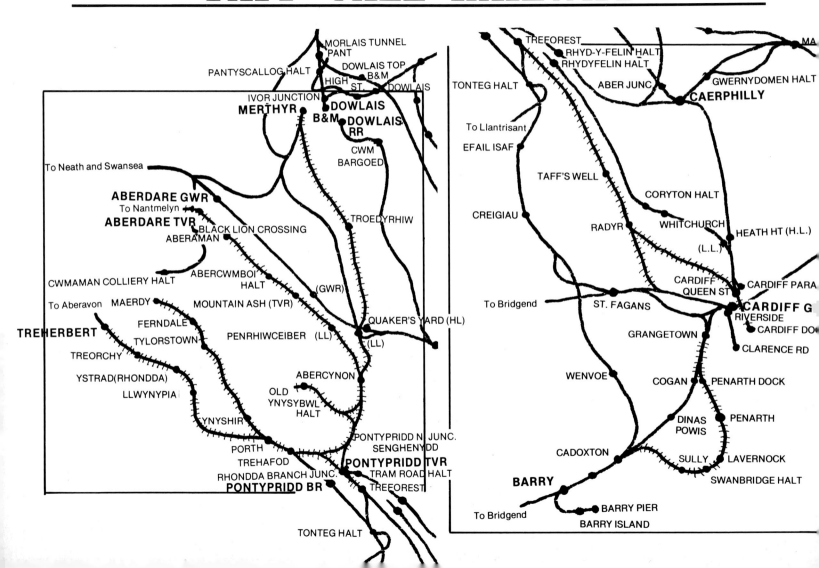

55 PENARTH DOCK STATION

Viewed looking in a north-west direction though Cardiff lay to the east of here. In the middle distance is Cogan Junction where the Barry Railway's lines joined those of the Taff Vale, the lines on the extreme right of the junction led down to Penarth Dock, the engine shed was situated just to the rear of the Down, or right hand platform, an engine can just be seen behind the waiting room on the down side, on one of the shed roads. From here, in the down direction, the notorious 1 in 40 gradient into Penarth started, often resulting in trains having to be banked between Cogan Junction and Penarth Town. To give some idea of the severity of this bank, the 1913 TVR Appendix gives details of goods and mineral trains that may travel over the section unassisted as follows:—

"In good weather the gross weight (including brakevan) must not exceed 82 tons for one engine."

"When rail and weather conditions are unfavourable, 50 tons for one engine."

To the rear right of the footbridge can be seen the TVR's Cogan Junction Signalbox which was later replaced by a GWR box though the former survived even after the signalling was taken over by the Cardiff Main Panel and the GWR box demolished.

56 LAVERNOCK STATION

Viewed looking in a north-easterly direction towards Penarth Town, the small mileage yard and goods shed lay to the right of the station. The line between Cogan Junction and Biglis Junction via Penarth was quite a tortuous route with gradients of 1 in 40 facing trains heading for Cadoxton, and 1 in 45 for those heading for Cogan though Lavernock Station was sited on the very easy 1 in 660 gradient that fell towards Penarth Town. The signalbox at Lavernock was situated at the Barry end of the station, the somersault bracket signal at the end of the Up, or left hand platform, just visible behind the footbridge, being the Outer Home for the Penarth Cement Works on the left and main line on the right. The decorative gable ends on the Down platform buildings are worthy of note, quite different from the usual pattern that adorned most Taff Vale buildings.

57 CARDIFF DOCKS *(Overleaf)*

Viewed looking north towards Queen Street Station, Cardiff Docks was the passenger terminus on the line from Queen Street, 1¼ miles distant, but goods traffic could go forward to various warehouses and sidings at the southern end of the docks. The Taff Vale Railway's West Yard Works were situated to the left of the photograph, the line at right angles to the main line, at the far end of the platform, led from a locomotive turntable at the right rear of the station, across Bute Street and into the aforementioned works; there were also two other rail crossings at Bute Street in close proximity to the one mentioned but the latter two were used for wagons, the West Yard pilot engine working this traffic. The first four wagons of the train on the left are a bit of a mixture belonging to the Taff Vale, Great Eastern, Midland and Great Western respectively. The large building on the extreme left of the picture was the original headquarters of the Taff Vale Railway until their removal to Queen Street station in 1862. The two buildings to the right of this building were used as workshops by the TVR but did not have rail access, whilst to the right of the train outside the station is Cardiff Terminus signalbox which not only controlled the main line but also engines and wagons going into the West Yard Works. Cardiff Docks station was authorised by the Board of Trade in 1879 up until such time the Taff Vale were using the site but without authorisation; passengers detrained by jumping from the carriages when the train stopped!

58 TREFOREST STATION

Viewed looking northwards towards Pontypridd, the small hut at the far end of the Down, or right hand platform being Treforest Ground Frame which worked the connection between the Up Goods line and Park sidings, the frame consisting of only two levers, the Up and Down goods lines lay to the rear of the Up platform as did the small goods yard. The majority of mineral traffic in the area was concentrated on Treforest Junction, 15 chains to the south of Treforest station, where the Barry Railway made connection with the Taff Vale. On the main platform buildings on the Down side the London & North Western Railway can be seen advertising the delights of Blackpool, probably only a dream to the majority of local inhabitants who made do with the beaches at Barry Island, Aberavon R&SB and later, Porthcawl.

59 PONTYPRIDD STATION

Viewed looking northwards towards Treherbert, the quadrupled track that had started at Cardiff ceased at the top end of the station where the lines branched for Treherbert and Abercynon. Pontypridd was an unusual station in that it made up of a number of bay platforms, one on the northern end of the Up platform, two built into the northern end of the station and two on this, the eastern side, of the station, through Down trains occupying the platform space between the two latter bays. The line going off to the right led to a pair of carriage sidings, whilst cattle traffic was handled in the pens that were situated on the far side of the running lines on the left of the picture, near enough directly opposite the photographer, their fate probably awaited them in the building on the extreme right, the local slaughterhouse!

60 PONTYPRIDD RHONDDA BRANCH JUNCTION

Viewed looking northwards from the two bay platforms let in to the top end of Pontypridd Station as already mentioned, lines for Treherbert and Maerdy lead off to the left while to the right are the lines for Ynysybwl, Aberdare, Merthyr and Nelson. This junction was at the southern end of a triangle, to its left, on the Treherbert line was Rhondda Cutting Junction and to the right, on the Merthyr line, Northern Junction, this enabled more use to be made of the cramped rail accommodation at Pontypridd Station in that passengers trains could be turned on the triangle and coal traffic not destined for one of the South Wales ports could be diverted to the north of the station.

61 PONTYPRIDD NORTHERN JUNCTION

Viewed looking in a westerly direction, the church in the right background is situated to the rear of the signalbox in the previous photograph, lines to the left lead into Pontypridd Station while those to the right head into the Rhondda Valley, note the home signal placed on the wrong side of the line for sighting purposes. Due to the severe curvature of the track on the Northern Curve, trains were restricted to 10 mph and due to the short length of the section trains of more than 25 wagons were not allowed into it unless the exit was clear. The winding gear visible in the left background belonged to Maritime Colliery, the sidings of which the Barry Railway passed over on their main line to Trehafod. An interesting working that used this curve was the Rio Tinto Copper traffic, when the Rhondda & Swansea Bay Railway opened their line to Treherbert in 1890 they worked the copper traffic to the latter where it was handed over to the Taff Vale who worked it forward to Merthyr, via Pontypridd Northern Junction, where it was handed over to the L&NWR who worked it to Abergavenny and Hereford. When the R&SB opened the Swansea Extension Railway in December 1894, and connected with the Cape Copper Works, even more of this lucrative traffic passed by this route. Some of it was worked forward from Merthyr by the B&M to Talyllyn Junction where it was handed over to either the Cambrian or the Midland Railway, depending upon the destination of the traffic.

62 TREHAFOD STATION

Viewed looking southwards towards Pontypridd, the Barry Railway having connected with the Taff Vale at Trehafod-Barry Junction, 13 chains to the south of the station, from where the former had running powers into Porth. At a later date, May 1919, these powers were extended to include the Ocean Collieries in the Rhondda Valley and to Ferndale, but only for a set amount of trains, three per day to each location. The goods yard and warehouse lay to the right of the station while just north of the station was Aerw Branch Junction where mineral trains for the Barry line were stopped at the Down Home signal for the purpose of picking up brakes in readiness for the climb from Trehafod-Barry Junction to just north of Pwllgwaun Goods depot, banking engines being supplied by Hafod Shed and later Coke Ovens for this section of 1 in 220 rising gradient. Meanwhile, Down mineral trains on the Taff Vale would be drifting down to Pontypridd on falling gradients of 1 in 175/256/220 and 277!

63 PORTH STATION

Viewed looking southwards towards Trehafod, the roof in the right foreground is that of Rhondda Fach Junction Signalbox, at the far end of the Up, or right hand platform is Porth Station Signalbox, these were later re-named Rhondda Fach North Junction Signalbox and Rhondda Fach Junction South Signalbox, the brick building just to the left of the telegraph pole in the right foreground was the original Porth Signalbox that was disused in 1883. The lines in the foreground are for the Maerdy Branch while those going to the right of the signalbox are for Treherbert. Note the pit in the siding at the top end of the Down platform, this was for the use of banking engines employed on the Maerdy Branch, mineral trains coming off the branch travelled on the Down relief, left hand track, being brought to a stand opposite the south box for the release of wagon brakes.

64 PORTH STATION

Viewed looking north towards Treherbert, Rhondda Fach Junction Signalbox is in the distance, left of centre, with the main line to Treherbert visible to the left of the box, Maerdy Branch to the right. The footbridge in the foreground was for access purposes and not for railway use, the goods yard at Porth was on the Maerdy Branch, there was also a mileage yard at Tynewydd Yard which was about $\frac{1}{4}$ mile north of Porth Station on the Down side of the Treherbert line, this was worked by Cymmer Level Signalbox. The building in the right foreground on the Down platform is nothing more than the Gents toilet, a similar structure adorned the Up platform.

65 YNYSHIR STATION

Viewed looking north towards Ferndale, Ynyshir being just under a mile distant from Porth but on a continuous rising gradient of 1 in 77 and 1 in 60 in fact, these were some of the easier gradients on the Maerdy Branch which had several sections of 1 in 55 which increased to 1 in 52 near the terminus! As can be seen, the platforms at Ynyshir were staggered, this being due to the close proximity of Ynyshir Standard Colliery, the rail entrance to which is opposite the northern end of the Down platform, the cross-over road can be seen beyond the footbridge, the section being under the control of Ynyshir Standard Signalbox that was situated on the Up side of the line, opposite the waiting room on the Down platform. The wagons stood in the background are in the Ynyshir Passing Siding which connects with the Down Relief just before the road overbridge, the northern end of this siding being under the control of the National Colliery Signalbox. When the siding was empty, and when necessary, it could be used for the working of goods and mineral trains in both directions. Note the Taff Vale standard outside framed oil lamp shed to the right of the photograph.

66 TYLORSTOWN STATION

Viewed looking southwards towards Ynyshir with a Barry Railway B1 Class 0-6-2T on a train of Up mineral empties being brought to a stand outside Tylorstown Signalbox, probably to the displeasure of the driver as the line here is on a rising gradient of 1 in 55! As mentioned earlier, in May 1919, the Barry Railway were given running powers to Ferndale, but only for three trains a day, the Taff Vale Railway were to supply a Pilot Driver and Guard, also a banking engine between Porth and Ferndale if needed. The goods yard at Tylorstown was at the far end of the station on the Up side but of interest in the photograph is the small gated mileage yard on the right of the picture, traffic for these yards was held at Porth until it was required at Tylorstown, the Station Master of which would advise Porth every morning of what traffic could be accepted.

67 FERNDALE STATION

Viewed looking north towards Maerdy and two miles on from Tylorstown. The goods shed and yard at Ferndale was situated to the rear of the photographer on the Up, or left hand side of the line, while the two road engine shed was to the north of the station, again, on the Up side. Opposite the shed stood Maerdy Junction Signalbox, the single line for the terminus turning away to the right while the left hand side of the junction led into D. Davis's Colliery where there were Pits Nos. 2 and 4, behind the photographer on the Down side, a branch went off to another of D. Davis's Collieries, where Pits Nos. 1 and 5 were situated. The signalbox in the right foreground is Ferndale Upper, Ferndale Lower being at the southern end of the goods yard on the Down side. Between Ferndale Upper Signalbox and Maerdy Junction Signalbox was Ferndale Upper Ground Frame, this was situated at the upper end of the Up Siding, north of the station, and worked the catch points and inlet points from the Up Main line.

68 MOUNTAIN ASH (OXFORD STREET) STATION

Viewed looking north towards Aberdare the line curving to the left after passing under the road bridge, the Great Western line to Aberdare was to the right, a semaphore signal and the road bridge over the line show how close it was to the Taff Vale line, being separated by the Afon Cynon. The chimney in the background belonged to the Deep Duffryn Colliery, the siding coming off the Down Main, or right hand track and disappearing behind the Down platform led to the Cambrian Wagon Works and Nixon's Navigation Colliery, both the collieries mentioned had extensive internal rail systems that made use of the sidings of both the TVR and GWR resulting in a rule that TVR trains setting back into Nixon's Siding had to be preceded by the Lower Duffryn Groundsman or, in his absence, the train guard to make certain that one of Nixon's locomotives were not at work in the same siding! Mountain Ash Station Signalbox was at the end of the Up platform and the small goods yard to the right of the Up platform, the covered loading bay of which is on the extreme left of the picture.

69 ABERCWMBOI HALT

Viewed looking northwards towards Aberdare, in various Taff Vale Working Time tables and Appendices it was spelt as Abercwmboy. In South Wales, stations with staggered platforms were not that uncommon, the usual reason for this being the close proximity of a colliery which, after all, was why the railway was there, but staggered halts such as Abercwmboi were extremely rare. The sidings beyond the Up platform were known as Middle Duffryn sidings, the signalbox of that name is just visible behind the somersault signal on the Down side. Powell Duffryn, owners of Middle Duffryn Colliery amongst others, had an extensive internal railway system in the area which connected with both the Taff Vale and the GWR just above Abercwmboi a mile north of which was Cwmbach Junction, the Taff Vale line to Aberdare carried on northwards whilst a branch went off to the right and crossed the GWR route to Aberdare in order to serve Werfa and Abernant Collieries, the branch was 51 chains in length.

70 ABERDARE STATION

Again viewed looking northwards with quite a good view of its unique platform canopy, 13 chains north of the station was Dare Valley Junction where one branch carried on to serve the Cynon Tinplate Works and the other drove westward to serve Bwllfa Dare Colliery passing under the Great Western's Gelli Tarw Junction to Cwmaman line in the process, from this latter branch, via Dare Junction, the GWR were also able to reach Bwllfa Dare Colliery. To the right of the picture can be seen one of the two locomotive sheds that the TVR had at Aberdare, both were two road sheds and in the same yard, the other being behind the photographer and to his right, the reason for there being two depots instead of one was the Afan Cynon that passed under the bridge at the top of the station and skirted round to the right of the yard making it impossible to construct a single shed of any sizeable dimension. A train of empty mineral wagons is just getting underway on the relief line, bound for Bwllfa Dare Colliery, $2\frac{1}{2}$ miles away, to the left of the picture is the two-road goods depot that adjoined the station and beyond the top end of the platform the Town Crossing Signalbox can just be seen, Aberdare South Signalbox being just beyond the Down end of the locomotive yard.

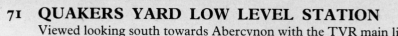

71 QUAKERS YARD LOW LEVEL STATION

Viewed looking south towards Abercynon with the TVR main line to the right and the GWR connection from their Branch Junction coming in on the left. The GWR and the TVR had signalboxes at Low Level Junction for the working of the same, the TVR signalbox being sited on the Up side of the line to the north of the station, the GWR High Level station was to the left of the photographer. Trains leaving Abercynon, just over 1½ miles to the south were faced with quite a formidable rising gradient of 1 in 40 towards Quakers Yard LL which eased to 1 in 281 some 350 yards south of the station and it was at Quakers Yard Station, in 1936, when South Wales was hit by freak gales, that the wooden refreshment room was lifted off the platform and deposited across the main line by the high winds.